THIS BOOK BELONGS TO:

_____

YOU MIGHT ALSO NEED

Cursive Handwriting Workbook for Adults:
Learning Cursive with Positive Affirmations & Inspirational Quotes

GET THE BOOK

OMG I Can't Remember:
Password Book with Usernames, Logins, Web Addresses, Email Addresses, PINs & Network Settings, A-Z

GET THE BOOK

YOU MIGHT ALSO NEED

The Print Handwriting Workbook for Kids:
Improve your Penmanship with 101 Interesting Science Facts

GET THE BOOK

The Print Handwriting Workbook for Teens:
Improve your Penmanship and Writing Skills with Motivational & Inspirational Quotes for Young Adults

GET THE BOOK

Introduction

Welcome to the *Small Print Handwriting Workbook for Adults!* This workbook is dedicated to adults seeking to refine their print penmanship while drawing inspiration from positive affirmations and motivational quotes. As we navigate the digital age, the timeless act of shaping each letter by hand holds a unique power – a craft that goes beyond ink and paper, reaching into the depths of our consciousness.

In this book, you'll find:
- 130+ pages filled with inspiring writing exercises for adults.
- College-ruled font size throughout the book.
- Unique dashed font, designed specially for handwriting practice, making it one of the best fonts for better handwriting.
- Easy and smooth penmanship practice despite the small font size.
- Clear, legible letters and bold ink.

Alphabet Practice:

Begin your handwriting practice by tracing and connecting the dots. Each letter is presented with directional arrows to guide the hand movements.

Uplifting Words:

Progress to tracing and copying uplifting words, starting with both uppercase and lowercase letters.

Affirmation Sentences:

The third part moves on to writing meaningful, uplifting affirmation sentences.

Motivational Quotes:

Continue practicing by writing motivational and stoic quotes from historical people such as Albert Einstein, Winston Churchill, Helen Keller, Seneca, Dale Carnegie, Mozart, and numerous others. The quotes progressively increase in length as you go on, and gives you the potential to enrich your wisdom along the way.

Reflection and Growth:

Conclude by answering introspective, open-ended questions using your improved penmanship - a testament to your growth on this handwriting journey.

It may seem tedious at first, but trust that print handwriting will help establish the tenacity that is important for the many learning experiences throughout your life. This book is our tribute to all of you grown-ups, who have taken an active part in your continuous growth!

SMALL PRINT HANDWRITING WORKBOOK FOR ADULTS:

Improve your Penmanship and Writing Skills with Positive Affirmations and Motivational Quotes

WHAT'S INSIDE?

A FEW TIPS:

- Good posture is essential during writing. Sitting upright will help with your writing efficiency.

- Pencils are softer and glide better on paper. You may likewise start practicing printing with ink pens once proficiency with the letters has been achieved.

- Be conscious of your pencil grip. Always make sure that the pad of your thumb touches your pen for easier, unrestricted writing motions.

- Feel free to cut out and copy any page in the book to continue your handwriting practice.

- Stay patient! Improving your handwriting is a journey of learning and growth. Remember, nothing of real value is ever easy.

UPPERCASE LETTERS

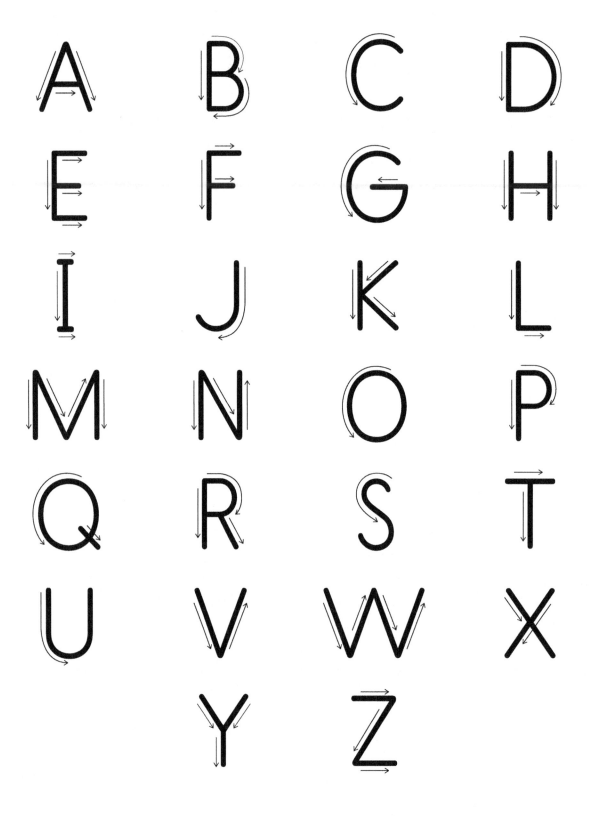

LOWERCASE LETTERS

a b c d

e f g h

i j k l

m n o p

q r s t

u v w x

y z

It had long since come to my attention that people of accomplishment rarely sat back and let things happen to them. They went out and happened to things.

- Leonardo da Vinci

Part 1:

Letters

Trace the dotted letters, then write the letters on your own.

A

a

B   B   B   B   B   B

B   B   B   B   B   B

B   B   B   B   B   B

B   B   B   B   B   B

B

B

B

B

b   b   b   b   b   b

b   b   b   b   b   b

b   b   b   b   b   b

b   b   b   b   b   b

b

b

b

b

b

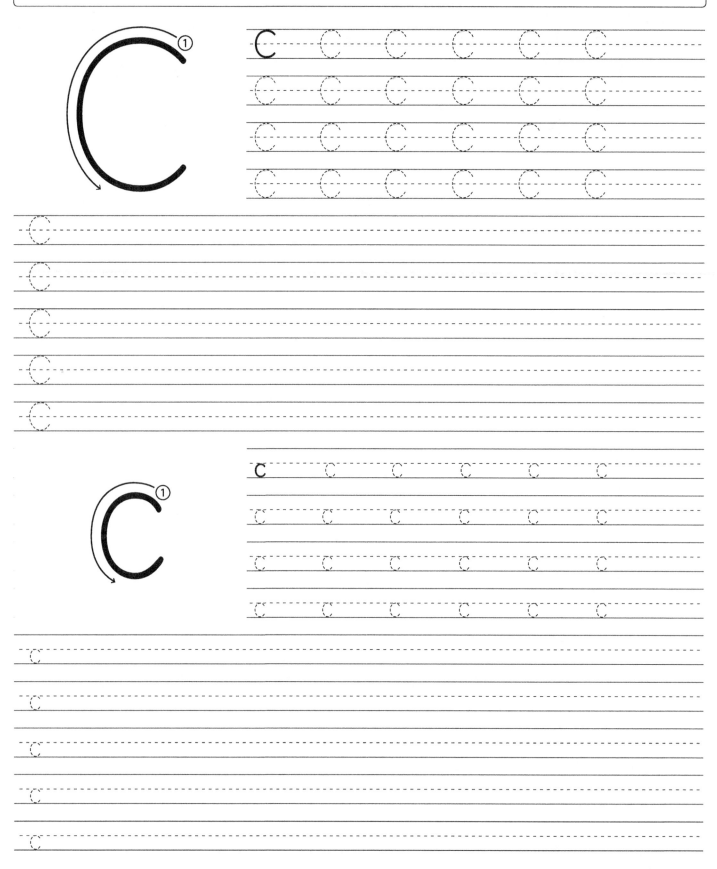

D

d

E E E E E E

e e e e e e

F

f

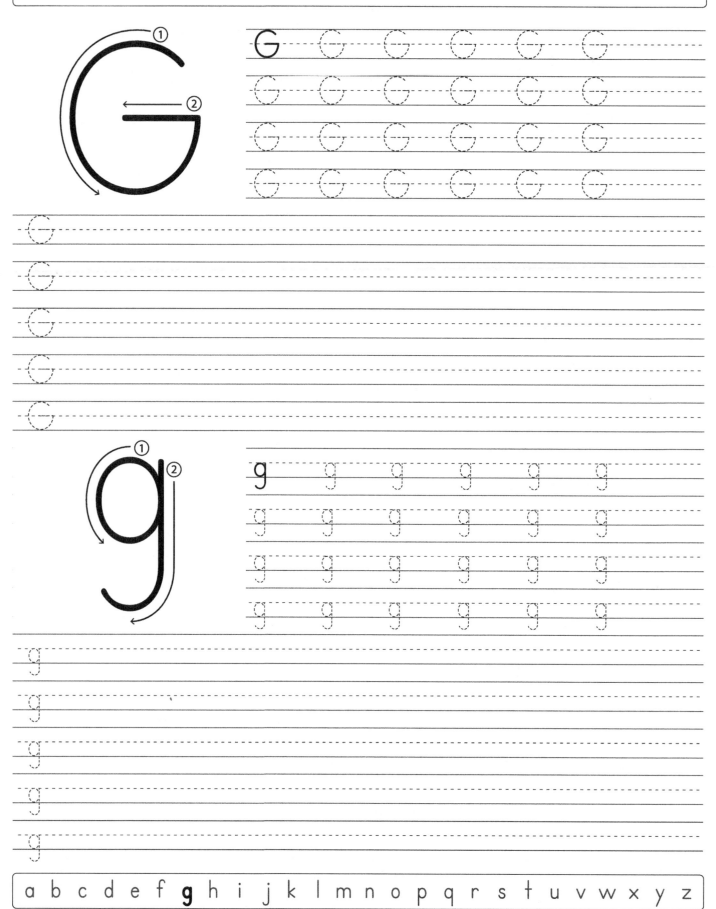

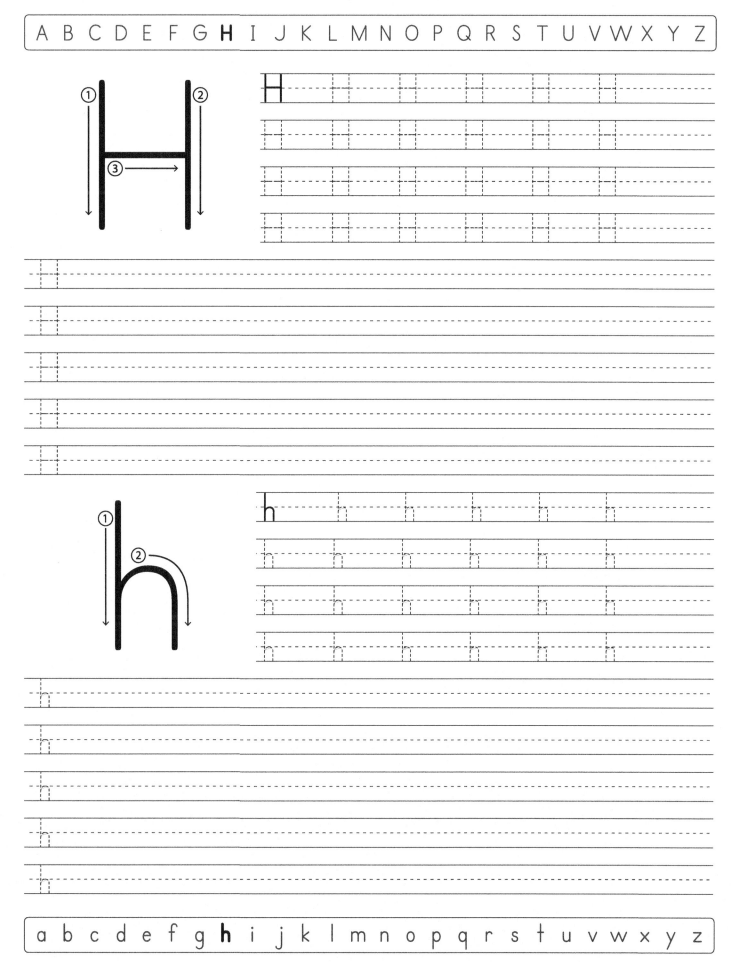

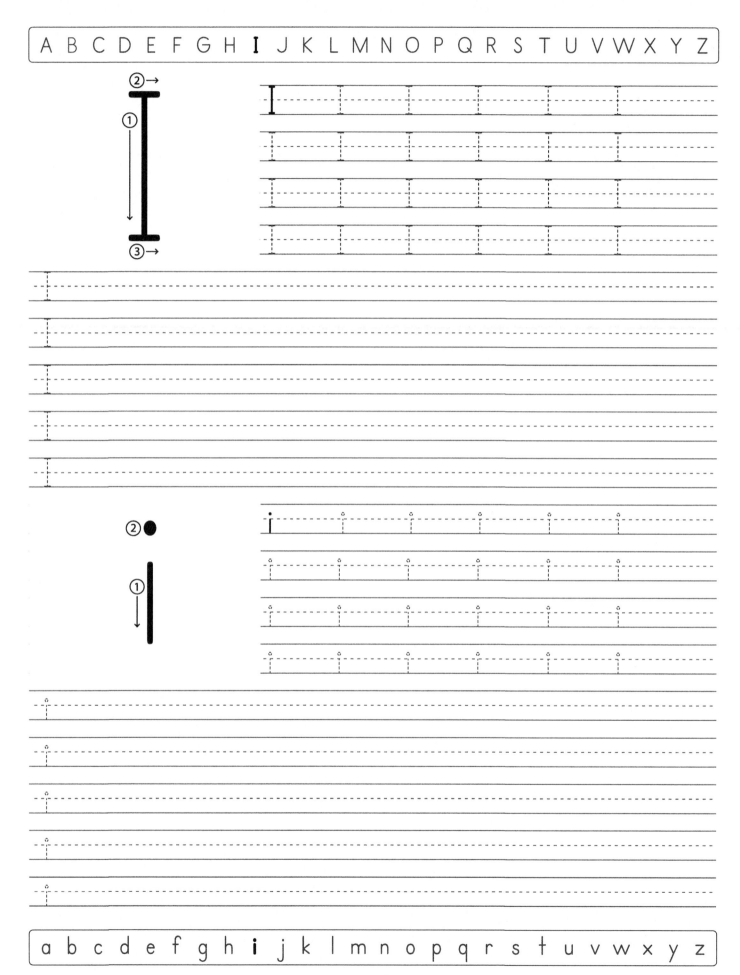

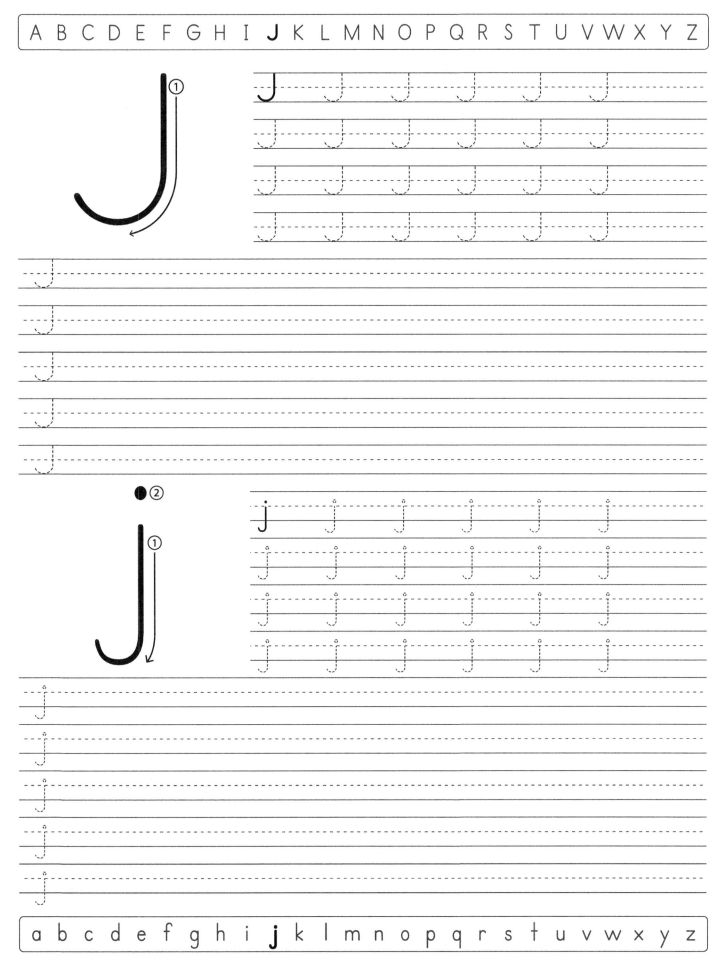

K

k

M M M M M M M
M M M M M M
M M M M M M
M M M M M M

M

M

M

M

M

m m m m m m m
m m m m m m
m m m m m m
m m m m m m

m

m

m

m

m

N N N N N N N

n n n n n n n

O

o

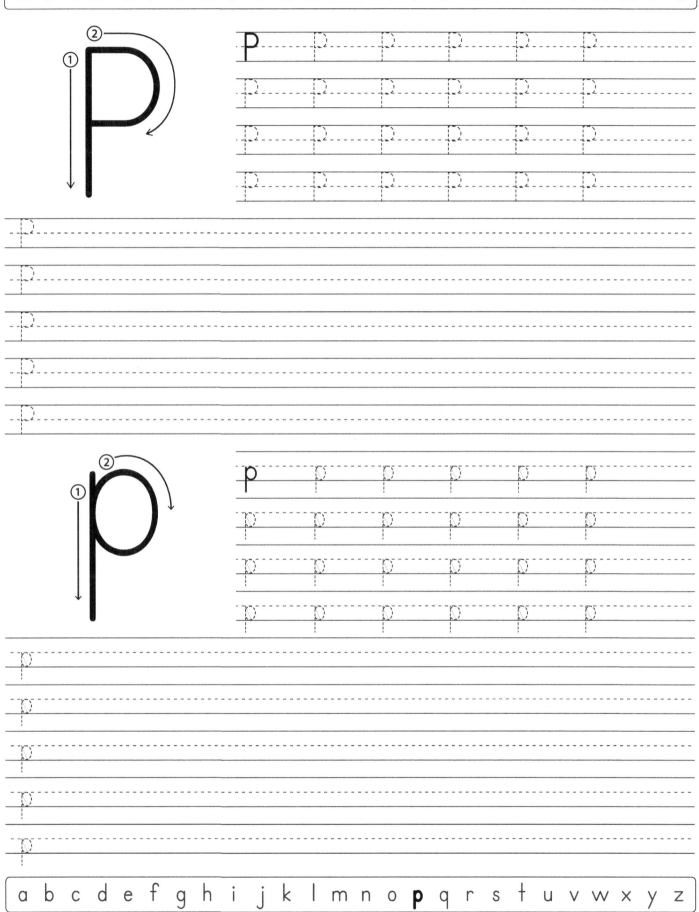

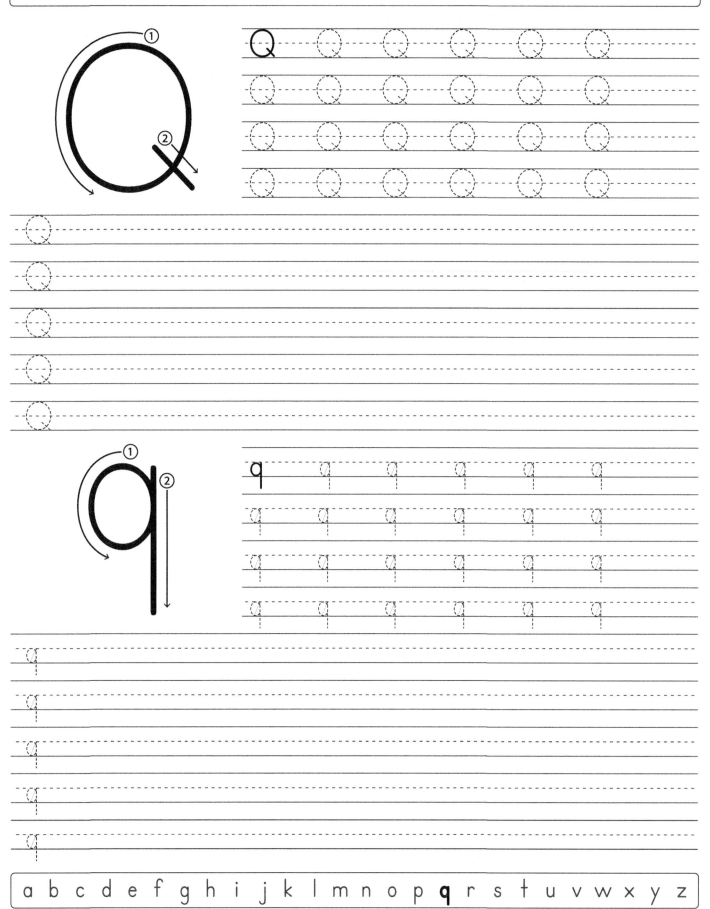

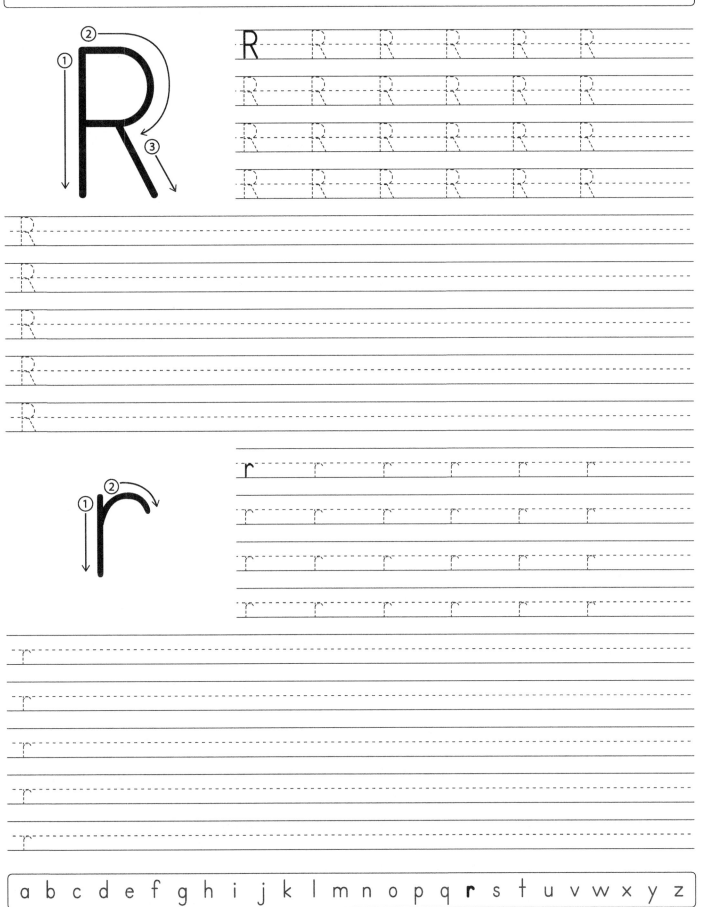

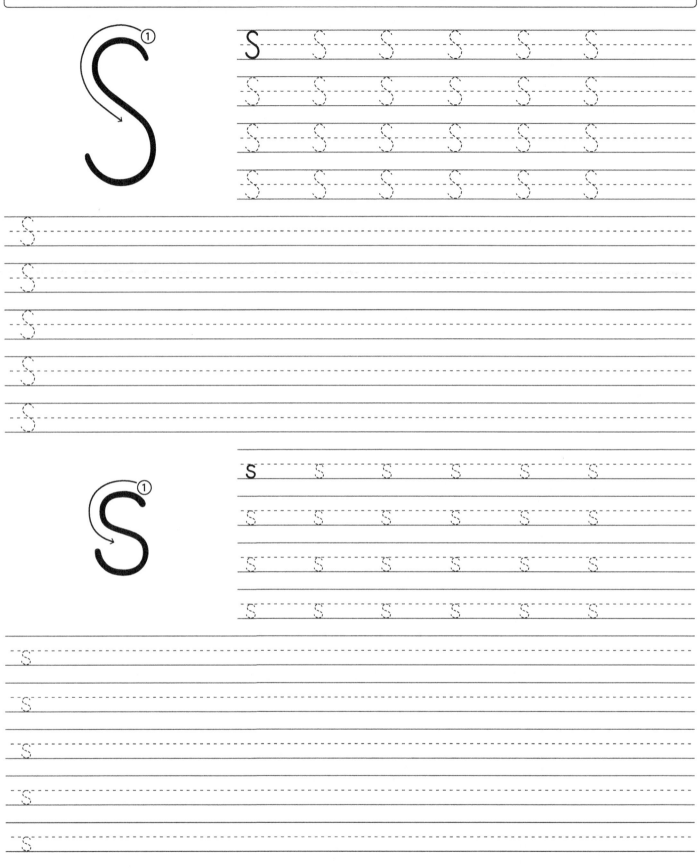

U

u

A B C D E F G H I J K L M N O P Q R S T U **V** W X Y Z

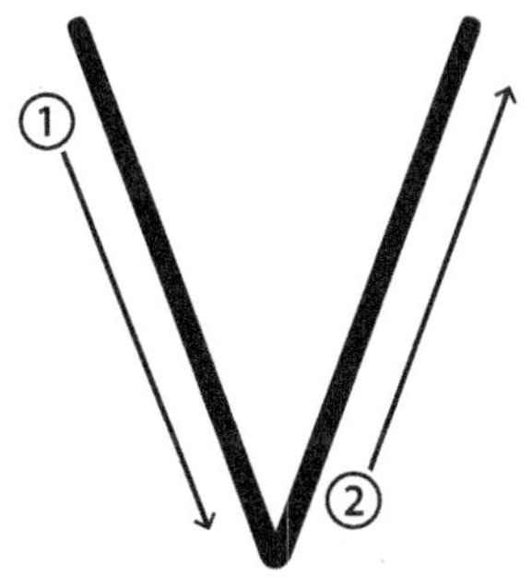

V

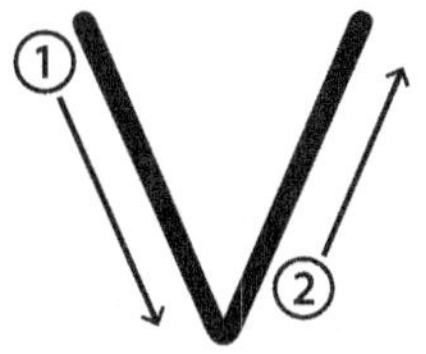

v

a b c d e f g h i j k l m n o p q r s t u **v** w x y z

A B C D E F G H I J K L M N O P Q R S T U V **W** X Y Z

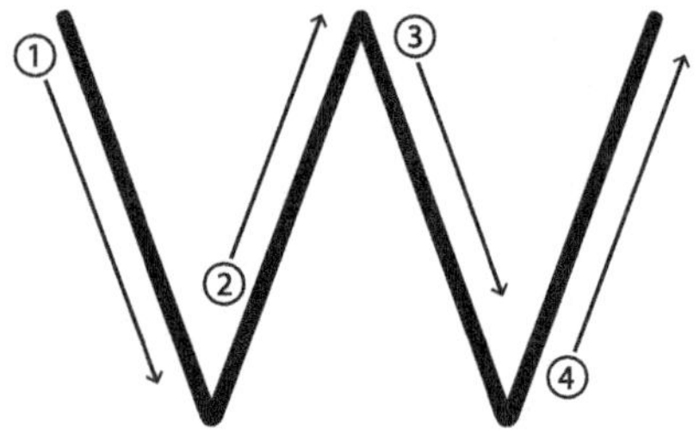

W W W W W W

W W W W W W

W W W W W W

W W W W W W

W

W

W

W

W

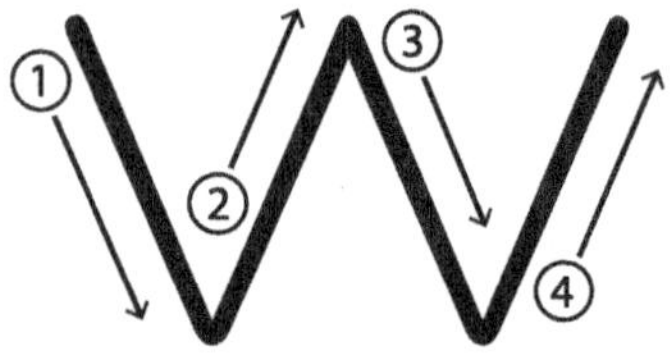

w w w w w w

w w w w w w

w w w w w w

w w w w w w

w

w

w

w

w

a b c d e f g h i j k l m n o p q r s t u v **w** x y z

A B C D E F G H I J K L M N O P Q R S T U V W **X** Y Z

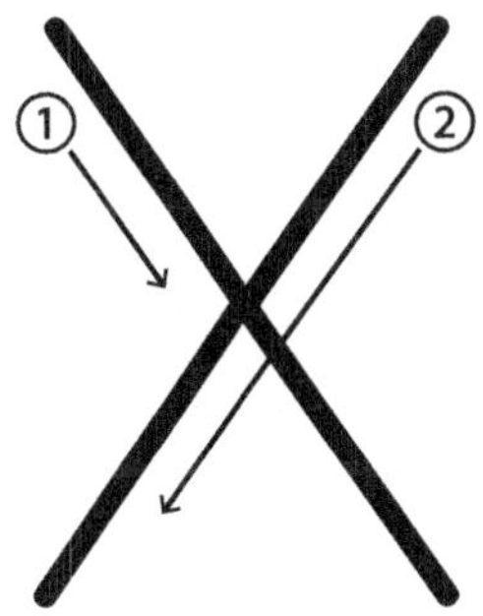

X X X X X X

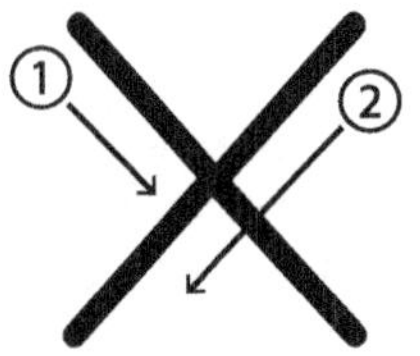

x x x x x x

a b c d e f g h i j k l m n o p q r s t u v w **x** y z

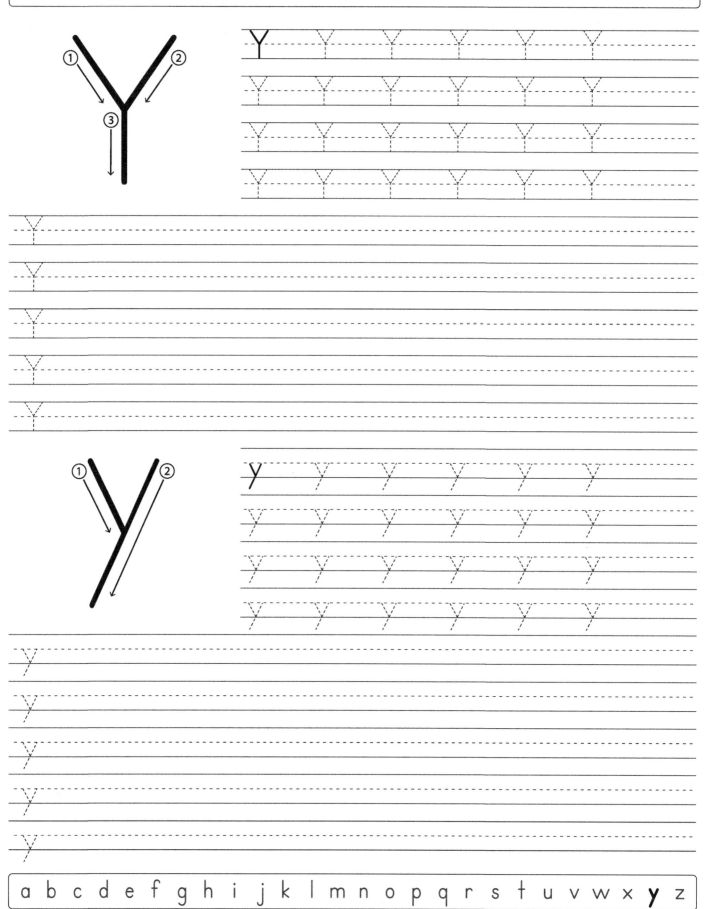

Z

z

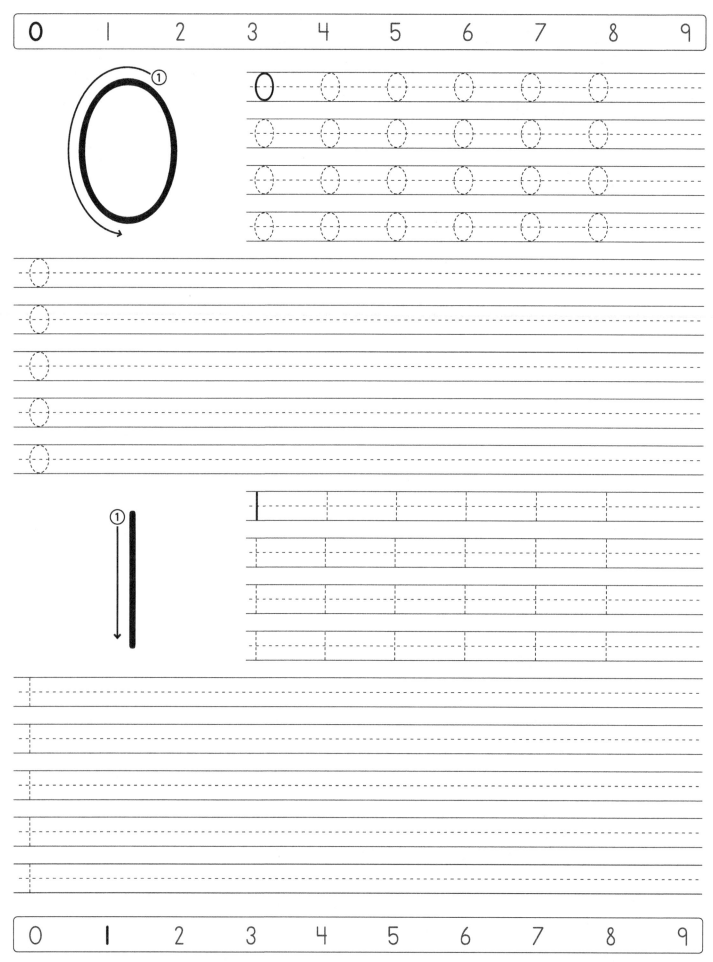

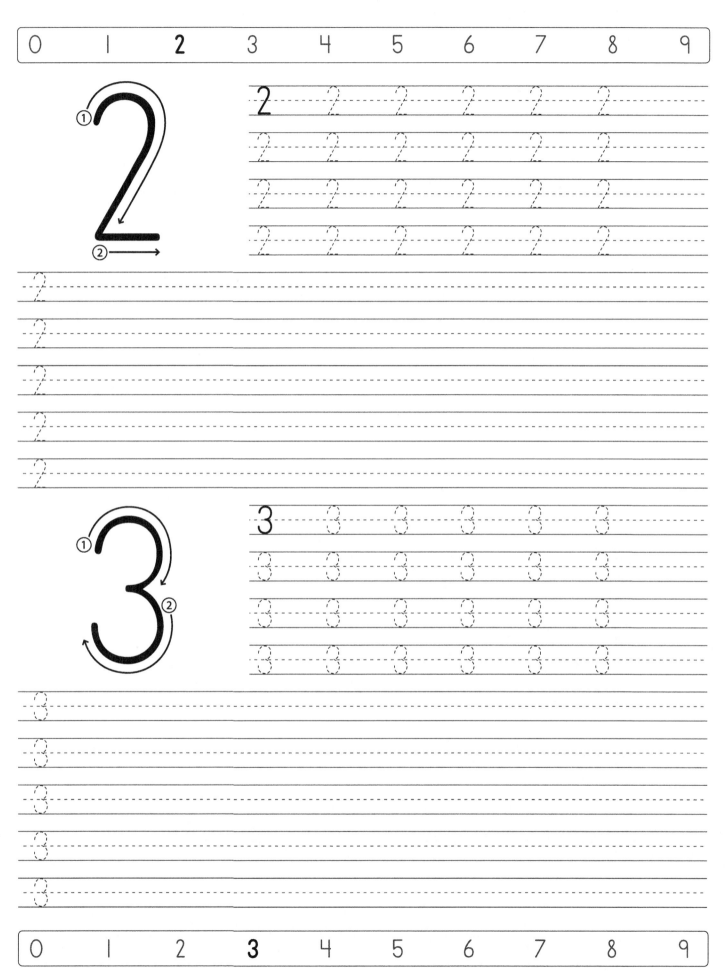

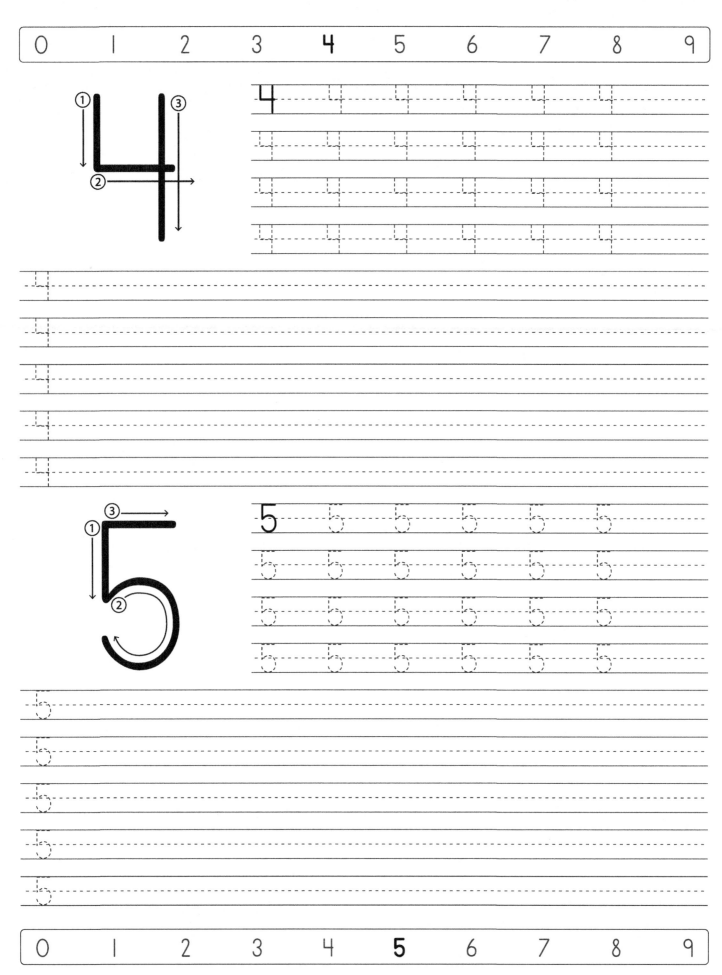

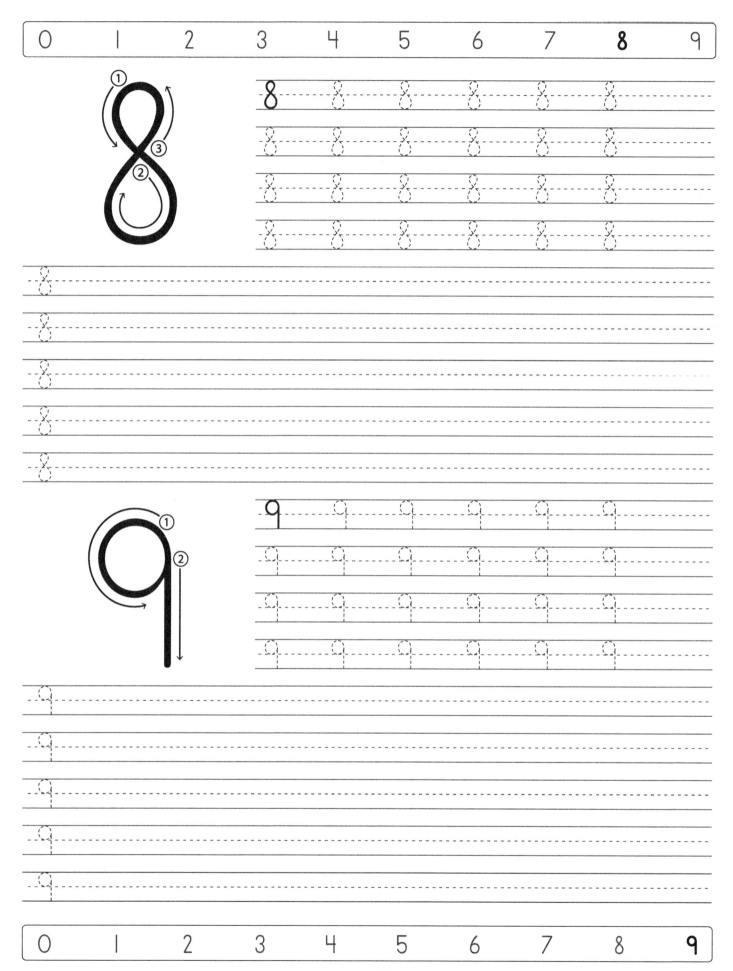

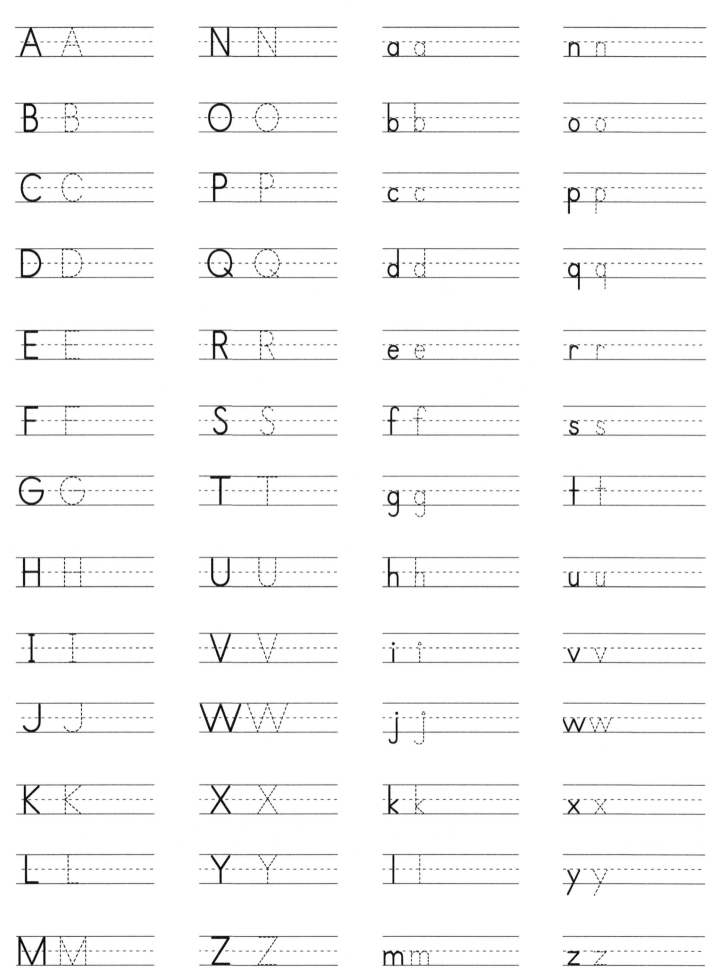

Part 2:

Words

Trace the dotted words,
then write the words on your own.

apex   apex   apex

be   be   be

calm   calm   calm

driven   driven   driven

easy   easy   easy

fine   fine   fine

glow   glow   glow

happy   happy   happy

inspire   inspire   inspire

joy   joy   joy

key   key   key

life   life   life

magic   magic   magic

now   now   now

oasis   oasis   oasis

pure   pure   pure

quiet   quiet   quiet

rise   rise   rise

spark   spark   spark

thrive   thrive   thrive

united   united   united

vision   vision   vision

wise   wise   wise

x-ray   x-ray   x-ray

yes   yes   yes

zebra   zebra   zebra

Write your own words here:

adore   adore   adore

Amazing   Amazing   Amazing

bright   bright   bright

Brave   Brave   Brave

charm   charm   charm

Creative   Creative   Creative

devoted   devoted   devoted

Discover   Discover   Discover

excited   excited   excited

Euphoria   Euphoria   Euphoria

flourish   flourish   flourish

Fearless   Fearless   Fearless

grateful   grateful   grateful

Genuine   Genuine   Genuine

humble   humble   humble

Harmony   Harmony   Harmony

impressive   impressive   impressive

Innovative   Innovative   Innovative

jaunt jaunt jaunt

Jelly Jelly Jelly

kind kind kind

Knowledge Knowledge Knowledge

laugh laugh laugh

Limitless Limitless Limitless

mindful mindful mindful

Motivation Motivation Motivation

nice nice nice

Natural Natural Natural

optimism optimism optimism

Outstanding Outstanding Outstanding

positive positive positive

Perseverance Perseverance Perseverance

quest quest quest

Quotidian Quotidian Quotidian

respect respect respect

Resilient Resilient Resilient

smile   smile   smile

Sunshine   Sunshine   Sunshine

thankful   thankful   thankful

Timeless   Timeless   Timeless

uplifting   uplifting   uplifting

Unstoppable   Unstoppable   Unstoppable

vibrant   vibrant   vibrant

Valiant   Valiant   Valiant

wonder   wonder   wonder

Welcoming Welcoming Welcoming

xenial xenial xenial

Xylophone Xylophone Xylophone

yearn yearn yearn

Yield Yield Yield

zestful zestful zestful

Zealous Zealous Zealous

Write your own words here:

46

Part 3:

Sentences

Trace the dotted sentences,
then write the sentences on your own.

I trust myself.   I trust myself.
I trust myself.   I trust myself.

Dreams fuel me.   Dreams fuel me.
Dreams fuel me.   Dreams fuel me.

I am unstoppable.   I am unstoppable.
I am unstoppable.   I am unstoppable.

I embrace my flaws.

I embrace my flaws.

My soul is at peace.

My soul is at peace.

My life is a blessing.

My life is a blessing.

Growth is my priority.

Growth is my priority.

Healing begins with me.

Healing begins with me.

Empathy is my strength.

Empathy is my strength.

Positivity is my mantra.

Positivity is my mantra.

I deserve a fresh start.

I deserve a fresh start.

I attract what I desire.

I attract what I desire.

My potential is limitless.
My potential is limitless.

I am a magnet for success.
I am a magnet for success.

Be the best version of you.
Be the best version of you.

Inner peace is my sanctuary.

Inner peace is my sanctuary.

I nourish my body every day.

I nourish my body every day.

Done is better than perfect.

Done is better than perfect.

We are all a work in progress.

We are all a work in progress.

Challenges are opportunities.

Challenges are opportunities.

I won't apologize for being me.

I won't apologize for being me.

Don't wish for it, work for it.

Don't wish for it, work for it.

I am worthy of love and respect.

I am worthy of love and respect.

I am the architect of my destiny.

I am the architect of my destiny.

Everything I want, wants me more.

Everything I want, wants me more.

Do good and good will come to you.

Do good and good will come to you.

Bad vibes don't go with my outfit.

Bad vibes don't go with my outfit.

You're valuable. Start acting like it.

You're valuable. Start acting like it.

My past does not determine my future.

My past does not determine my future.

My handwriting is improving every day.

My handwriting is improving every day.

Be loyal to your future, not your past.

Be loyal to your future, not your past.

So many exciting things are ahead of me.

So many exciting things are ahead of me.

Forget perfection and focus on progress.

Forget perfection and focus on progress.

Slow progress is better than no progress.

Slow progress is better than no progress.

I am improving my study habits every day.

I am improving my study habits every day.

Every situation is easy for me to handle.

Every situation is easy for me to handle.

Once you choose hope, anything is possible.

Once you choose hope, anything is possible.

My happy thoughts help create my healthy body.

My happy thoughts help create my healthy body.

Everything is working out for my highest good.

Everything is working out for my highest good.

My immune system is strong and will protect me.

I have all that I need to get through today.

I accept my failures, as they don't define me.

Doubt kills more dreams than failure ever will.

Doubt kills more dreams than failure ever will.

You are the author of your story, write it well.

You are the author of your story, write it well.

Good things will come to those in my life today.

Good things will come to those in my life today.

A beautiful day begins with a beautiful
mindset.

A beautiful day begins with a beautiful
mindset.

A little progress each day adds up to
big results.

A little progress each day adds up to
big results.

The beauty of handwriting lies within
its uniqueness.

The beauty of handwriting lies within
its uniqueness.

My only competitor is the person I was
yesterday.

My only competitor is the person I was
yesterday.

Beauty begins the moment you decide to
be yourself.

Beauty begins the moment you decide to
be yourself.

Never stop learning because life never
stops teaching.

Never stop learning because life never
stops teaching.

Calming thoughts will fill my mind
as I sleep tonight.

Calming thoughts will fill my mind
as I sleep tonight.

All is well in my world. I am calm,
happy and content.

All is well in my world. I am calm,
happy and content.

Congrats. You woke up again today.
Make the most of it.

Congrats. You woke up again today.
Make the most of it.

You're capable of way more than you're

currently doing.

You're capable of way more than you're

currently doing.

When you feel like quitting, think about

why you started.

When you feel like quitting, think about

why you started.

Each day, I am growing stronger, wiser,

and more resilient.

Each day, I am growing stronger, wiser,

and more resilient.

Every day I will focus on caring for
myself, as much as I care for others.

Every day I will focus on caring for
myself, as much as I care for others.

Make your vision so clear that your
fears become irrelevant.

Make your vision so clear that your
fears become irrelevant.

I embrace the joy of improving my
handwriting, one stroke at a time.

I embrace the joy of improving my
handwriting, one stroke at a time.

Life is 10% what happens to you, and 90%
how you react to it.

Life is 10% what happens to you, and 90%
how you react to it.

You are everything you think you are, so
choose your thoughts wisely.

You are everything you think you are, so
choose your thoughts wisely.

Every day, in every way, I am becoming a
better version of myself.

Every day, in every way, I am becoming a
better version of myself.

Part 4:

Quotes

Trace the dotted quotes,
then write the quotes on your own.

"I have not failed. I've just found
10,000 ways that won't work."

- Thomas Edison

I have not failed. I've just found 10,000 ways
that won't work.

I have not failed. I've just found 10,000 ways
that won't work.

"When it rains, look for rainbows.
When it's dark, look for stars."
- Oscar Wilde

When it rains, look for rainbows.
When it's dark, look for stars.
When it rains, look for rainbows.
When it's dark, look for stars.

"Never engage in a battle of wits
with an unarmed man."

- Sir Winston Churchill

Never engage in a battle of wits with an

unarmed man.

Never engage in a battle of wits with an

unarmed man.

"Stay away from negative people, they have a problem for every solution."

– Albert Einstein

Stay away from negative people, they have a

problem for every solution.

Stay away from negative people, they have a

problem for every solution.

"The future belongs to those who believe in the beauty of their dreams."

– Eleanor Roosevelt

The future belongs to those who believe in the
beauty of their dreams.

The future belongs to those who believe
in the beauty of their dreams.

"Success is the ability to go from failure to
failure without losing your enthusiasm."
- Sir Winston Churchill

Success is the ability to go from failure to failure
without losing your enthusiasm.
Success is the ability to go from failure to failure
without losing your enthusiasm.

"One day, in retrospect, the years of struggle will strike you as the most beautiful."

– Sigmund Freud

One day, in retrospect, the years of struggle will strike you as the most beautiful.

One day, in retrospect, the years of struggle will strike you as the most beautiful.

"We are more often frightened than hurt; and we suffer more in imagination than in reality."

- Seneca

We are more often frightened than hurt; and we
suffer more in imagination than in reality.
We are more often frightened than hurt; and we
suffer more in imagination than in reality.

"Give me six hours to chop down a tree and
I will spend the first four sharpening the axe."

- Abraham Lincoln

Give me six hours to chop down a tree and
I will spend the first four sharpening the axe.
Give me six hours to chop down a tree and
I will spend the first four sharpening the axe.

"The secret of change is to focus all of your energy, not on fighting the old, but on building the new."

– Socrates

The secret of change is to focus all of your energy, not on fighting the old, but on building the new.

The secret of change is to focus all of your energy, not on fighting the old, but on building the new.

"I alone cannot change the world, but I can cast a stone across the water to create many ripples."

- Mother Teresa

I alone cannot change the world, but I can cast a stone across the water to create many ripples.

I alone cannot change the world, but I can cast a stone across the water to create many ripples.

"When you are content to be simply yourself
and don't compare or compete, everyone will
respect you."
- Lao Tzu

When you are content to be simply yourself
and don't compare or compete, everyone will
respect you.

"Our greatest weakness lies in giving up.
The most certain way to succeed is always
to try just one more time."

- Thomas Edison

Our greatest weakness lies in giving up.
The most certain way to succeed is always to
try just one more time.

"I can't give you the formula for success,
but I can give you a formula for failure:
try to please everybody all the time."

— Herbert Bayard Swope

I can't give you the formula for success, but I can
give you a formula for failure: try to please
everybody all the time.

"Hope is the thing with feathers, that perches in the soul, and sings the tune without the words, and never stops at all."

– Emily Dickinson

Hope is the thing with feathers, that perches in
the soul, and sings the tune without the words,
and never stops at all.

"Smart people learn from everything and everyone, average people from their experiences, stupid people already have all the answers."

\- Socrates

Smart people learn from everything and everyone, average people from their experiences, stupid people already have all the answers.

"Never let the future disturb you. You will meet it, if you have to, with the same weapons of reason which today arm you against the present."

- Marcus Aurelius

Never let the future disturb you. You will meet it, if you have to, with the same weapons of reason which today arm you against the present.

"If you can't fly then run, if you can't run then walk, if you can't walk then crawl, but whatever you do you have to keep moving forward."

- Martin Luther King Jr.

If you can't fly then run, if you can't run then
walk, if you can't walk then crawl, but whatever
you do you have to keep moving forward.

"Most of the important things in the world have been accomplished by people who have kept on trying when there seemed to be no hope at all."

- Dale Carnegie

Most of the important things in the world have
been accomplished by people who have kept on
trying when there seemed to be no hope at all.

"When we hate our enemies, we are giving them power over us: power over our sleep, our appetites, our blood pressure, our health, and our happiness."

- Dale Carnegie

When we hate our enemies, we are giving them
power over us: power over our sleep, our appetites,
our blood pressure, our health, and our happiness.

"If you are depressed you are living in the past. If you are anxious you are living in the future. If you are at peace you are living in the present."

- Lao Tzu

If you are depressed you are living in the past.
If you are anxious you are living in the future.
If you are at peace you are living in the present.

"Keep away from people who try to belittle your ambitions. Small people always do that, but the really great make you feel that you, too, can become great."

- Mark Twain

Keep away from people who try to belittle your
ambitions. Small people always do that, but the
really great make you feel that you, too, can
become great.

"When one door of happiness closes, another opens. But often we look so long at the closed door that we do not see the one which has been opened for us."

– Helen Keller

When one door of happiness closes, another opens. But often we look so long at the closed door that we do not see the one which has been opened for us.

"It had long since come to my attention that people of accomplishment rarely sat back and let things happen to them. They went out and happened to things."

– Leonardo da Vinci

It had long since come to my attention that
people of accomplishment rarely sat back and
let things happen to them. They went out and
happened to things.

"Everything can be taken from a man but one thing: the last of the human freedoms—to choose one's attitude in any given set of circumstances, to choose one's own way."

- Viktor Frankl

Everything can be taken from a man but one thing: the last of the human freedoms—to choose one's attitude in any given set of circumstances, to choose one's own way.

"You can make more friends in two months by becoming interested in other people than you can in two years by trying to get other people interested in you."

– Dale Carnegie

You can make more friends in two months by becoming interested in other people than you can in two years by trying to get other people interested in you.

"When I was a boy of 14, my father was so ignorant I could hardly stand to have the old man around. But when I got to be 21, I was astonished at how much the old man had learned in seven years."

– Mark Twain

When I was a boy of 14, my father was so ignorant I could hardly stand to have the old man around. But when I got to be 21, I was astonished at how much the old man had learned in seven years.

"If you accomplish something good with hard work, the labor passes quickly, but the good endures. If you do something shameful in pursuit of pleasure, the pleasure passes quickly, but the shame endures."

– Gaius Musonius Rufus

If you accomplish something good with hard work, the labor passes quickly, but the good endures. If you do something shameful in pursuit of pleasure, the pleasure passes quickly, but the shame endures.

"If anyone tells you that a certain person speaks ill of you, do not make excuses about what is said of you but answer, 'he was ignorant of my other faults, else he would not have mentioned these alone.'"

– Epictetus

If anyone tells you that a certain person speaks ill of you, do not make excuses about what is said of you but answer, "he was ignorant of my other faults, else he would not have mentioned these alone."

"All I insist on, and nothing else, is that you should show the whole world that you are not afraid. Be silent, if you choose; but when it is necessary, speak and speak in such a way that people will remember it."

- Wolfgang Amadeus Mozart

All I insist on, and nothing else, is that you should show the whole world that you are not afraid. Be silent, if you choose; but when it is necessary, speak and speak in such a way that people will remember it.

"Some of us have great runways already built for us. If you have one, take off. But if you don't have one, realize it is your responsibility to grab a shovel and build one for yourself and for those who will follow after you."

– Amelia Earhart

Some of us have great runways already built for us.
If you have one, take off. But if you don't have one,
realize it is your responsibility to grab a shovel and
build one for yourself and for those who will follow
after you.

"Everybody in the world is seeking happiness and there is one sure way to find it. That is by controlling your thoughts. Happiness doesn't depend on outward conditions. It depends on inner conditions."

– Dale Carnegie

Everybody in the world is seeking happiness and there is one sure way to find it. That is by controlling your thoughts. Happiness doesn't depend on outward conditions. It depends on inner conditions.

"To accuse others for one's own misfortune is a sign of want of education. To accuse oneself shows that one's education has begun. To accuse neither oneself nor others shows that one's education is complete."

– Epictetus

To accuse others for one's own misfortune is a sign of want of education. To accuse oneself shows that one's education has begun. To accuse neither oneself nor others shows that one's education is complete.

"When I am completely myself, entirely alone or during the night when I cannot sleep, it is on such occasions that my ideas flow best and most abundantly. Whence and how these ideas come I know not, nor can I force them."

– Wolfgang Amadeus Mozart

When I am completely myself, entirely alone or during the night when I cannot sleep, it is on such occasions that my ideas flow best and most abundantly. Whence and how these ideas come I know not, nor can I force them.

"If someone is able to show me that what I think or do is not right, I will happily change, for I seek the truth, by which no one was ever truly harmed. It is the person who continues in his self-deception and ignorance who is harmed."

– Marcus Aurelius

If someone is able to show me that what I think or do is not right, I will happily change, for I seek the truth, by which no one was ever truly harmed. It is the person who continues in his self-deception and ignorance who is harmed.

"Everyone should consider his body as a priceless gift from one whom he loves above all, a marvelous work of art, of indescribable beauty, and mystery beyond human conception, and so delicate that a word, a breath, a look, nay, a thought may injure it."

– Nikola Tesla

Everyone should consider his body as a priceless
gift from one whom he loves above all, a
marvelous work of art, of indescribable beauty,
and mystery beyond human conception, and so
delicate that a word, a breath, a look, nay,
a thought may injure it.

"When I was five years old, my mom always told me that happiness was the key to life. When I went to school, they asked me what I wanted to be when I grew up. I wrote down "happy". They told me I didn't understand the assignment and I told them they didn't understand life."

– Gaius Julius Caesar

When I was five years old, my mom always told me that happiness was the key to life. When I went to school, they asked me what I wanted to be when I grew up. I wrote down "happy". They told me I didn't understand the assignment and I told them they didn't understand life.

"You will never have a greater or lesser dominion than that over yourself. The height of a man's success is gauged by his self-mastery; the depth of his failure by his self-abandonment. And this law is the expression of eternal justice. He who cannot establish dominion over himself will have no dominion over others."

– Leonardo da Vinci

You will never have a greater or lesser dominion than that over yourself. The height of a man's success is gauged by his self-mastery; the depth of his failure by his self-abandonment. And this law is the expression of eternal justice. He who cannot establish dominion over himself will have no dominion over others.

Part 5:

Activities

Answer the open-ended questions with your improved handwriting.

What affirmations or quotes resonate with you the most and why?

How do you prioritize self-care and nourishment for your mind, body, and spirit?

If you could change something in your life, what would it be?

What experiences or moments bring you the most joy and contentment in your life?

What are your goals and aspirations?
How do you plan to achieve them in the
near future?

What are five things you currently do that contribute to your productivity, happiness, and success?

Reflect on your handwriting progress
and describe its impact on you.
What progress have you made?

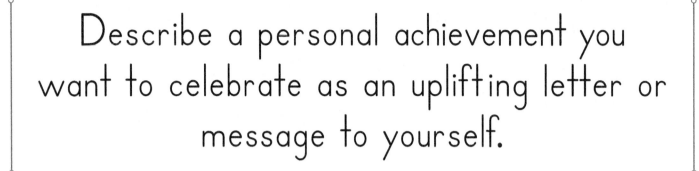

Describe a personal achievement you want to celebrate as an uplifting letter or message to yourself.

Reflecting on your journey thus far, how can you ensure your life reflects your passions, purpose, and values, leaving a meaningful legacy for yourself and others?

Hi there! This book was created just for you, to help you improve your print handwriting in a fun and meaningful way. We would love to hear about it as you write a short review on Amazon, it could really help us.

Create Review

If you have any questions about this book, please feel free to contact Leslie Mars at:

Lesliemarsbooks@gmail.com

Printed in Great Britain
by Amazon

40542357R00077